Air Fryer Cookbook for Beginners

A Beginner's Cookbook with Delicious and Easy Recipes.
Save Money and Time with Delicious, Amazing and Mouth-watering Dishes.

Ursula Mayert

Table of Contents

Furthermore, the transmission, duplication, or reproduction of any of the following work including specific information will be considered an illegal act irrespective of if it is done electronically or in print. This extends to creating a secondary or tertiary copy of the work or a recorded copy and is only allowed with the express written consent from the Publisher. All additional right reserved.

The information in the following pages is broadly considered a truthful and accurate account of facts and as such, any inattention, use, or misuse of the information in question by the reader will render any resulting actions solely under their purview. There are no scenarios in which the publisher or the original author of this work can be in any fashion deemed liable for any hardship or damages that may befall them after undertaking information described herein.

Additionally, the information in the following pages is intended only for informational purposes and should thus be thought of as universal. As befitting its nature, it is presented without assurance regarding its prolonged validity or interim quality. Trademarks that are mentioned are done without written consent and can in no way be considered an endorsement from the trademark holder.

Introduction

An air fryer is a relatively new kitchen appliance that has proven to be very popular among consumers. While there are many different varieties available, most air fryers share many common features. They all have heating elements that circulate hot air to cook the food. Most come with pre-programmed settings that assist users in preparing a wide variety of foods. Air frying is a healthier style of cooking because it uses less oil than traditional deep frying methods. While it preserves the flavor and quality of the food, it reduces the amount of fat used in cooking. Air frying is a common method for "frying" foods that are primarily made with eggs and flour. These foods can be soft or crunchy to your preference by using this method.

How air fryers work

Air fryers use a blower to circulate hot air around food. The hot air heats the moisture on the food until it evaporates and creates steam. As steam builds up around the food, it creates pressure that pulls moisture from the surface of the food and pushes it away from the center, forming small bubbles. The bubbles creates a layer of air that surrounds the food and creates a crispy crust.

Choosing an air fryer

When choosing an air fryer, look for one that has good reviews for customer satisfaction. Start with the features you need, such as power, capacity size and accessories. Look for one that is easy to use. Some air fryers on the market have a built-in timer and adjustable temperature. Look for one with a funnel to catch grease, a basket that is dishwasher-safe and parts that are easy to clean.

How To Use An Air Fryer

For best results, preheat the air fryer at 400 F for 10 minutes. Preheating the air fryer allows it to reach the right temperature faster. In addition, preheating the air fryer is essential to ensure that your food won't burn.

How to cook stuff in an Air Fryer

If you don't have an air fryer yet, you can start playing with your ovens by throwing some frozen fries in there and cooking them until they are browned evenly. Depending on your oven, take a look at the temperature. You may need to increase or decrease the time.

What Foods Can You Cook In An Air Fryer?

Eggs: While you can cook eggs in an air fryer, we don't recommend it because you can't control the cooking time and temperature as precisely as with a traditional frying pan or skillet. It's much easier to get unevenly cooked eggs. You also can't toss in any sauces or seasonings and you won't get crispy, golden brown edges.

Frozen foods: Generally, frozen foods are best cooked in the conventional oven because they need to reach a certain temperature to be properly cooked. The air fryer is not capable of reaching temperatures that result in food being fully cooked.

Dehydrated Foods: Dehydrated foods require deep-frying, which is not something you can do with an air fryer. When it comes to cooking dehydrated foods, the air fryer is not the best option.

Vegetables: You can cook vegetables in an air fryer but you have to make sure that the air fryer is not set at a temperature that will burn them.

To ensure that your vegetables aren't overcooked, start the air fryer with the basket off, then toss in the veggies once the air has heated up and there are no more cold spots.

Make sure to stir the vegetables every few minutes. Cooking them in the basket is also an option, but they may stick together a little bit.

Fries: Frying fries in an air fryer is a good way to get crispy, golden-brown fries without adding lots of oil. Compared to conventional frying, air frying yields fewer calories.

To cook french fries in an air fryer, use a basket or a rack and pour in enough oil to come about halfway up the height of the fries. For best results, make sure the fries are frozen. Turn the air fryer onto 400 degrees and set it for 12 minutes. If you want them extra crispy, you can set it for 18 minutes, but they may burn a bit.

Benefits of an air fryer:

• It's one of the easiest ways to cook healthy foods. Used 4-5 times a week, it's a healthier option than frying with oil in your conventional oven or using canned foods.

• Air fryer meals are an easy way to serve tasty food that doesn't take up lots of space. Air fryers make it possible to cook three times as much food as you can in your microwave.

• Air fryers have a small footprint and you can store them away in a cabinet when not in use.

•They are versatile kitchen appliances. You can use them to cook food for lunch, dinner and snacks.

• Air fryers require little to no fussing in the kitchen. You can use them with the lid on, which means there's less washing up to do.

Garlic Putter Pork Chops

Preparation Time: 10 minutes

Cooking Time: 10 minutes

Servings: 4

Ingredients:

- tsp. parsley
- tsp. grated garlic cloves
- 1 tbsp. coconut oil
- 1 tbsp. coconut butter
- pork chops

Directions:

1. Preparing the Ingredients. Ensure your air fryer is preheated to 350 degrees.
2. Mix butter, coconut oil, and all seasoning together. Then rub seasoning mixture over all sides of pork chops. Place in foil, seal, and chill for 1 hour.
3. Remove pork chops from foil and place into air fryer.
4. Air Frying. Set temperature to 350°F, and set time to 7 minutes. Cook 7 minutes on one side and 8 minutes on the other.
5. Drizzle with olive oil and serve alongside a green salad.

Nutrition:

Calories: 526;

Fat: 23g;

Protein:41g;

Sugar:4g

Cajun Pork Steaks

Preparation Time: 5 minutes

Cooking Time: 20 minutes

Servings: 6

Ingredients:

- 4-6 pork steaks
- BBQ sauce:
- Cajun seasoning
- 1 tbsp. vinegar
- 1 tsp. low-sodium soy sauce
- ½ C. brown sugar

Directions:

1   Preparing the Ingredients. Ensure your air fryer is preheated to 290 degrees.

2   Sprinkle pork steaks with Cajun seasoning.

3   Combine remaining ingredients and brush onto steaks. Add coated steaks to air fryer.

4   Air Frying. Set temperature to 290°F, and set time to 20 minutes. Cook 15-20 minutes till just browned.

Nutrition:

Calories: 209;

Fat: 11g;

Protein:28g;

Sugar:2g

Cajun Sweet-Sour Grilled Pork

Preparation Time: 5 minutes

Cooking Time: 12 minutes

Servings: 3

Ingredients:

- ¼ cup brown sugar
- 1/4 cup cider vinegar
- 1-lb pork loin, sliced into 1-inch cubes
- tablespoons Cajun seasoning
- tablespoons brown sugar

Directions:

1 Preparing the Ingredients. In a shallow dish, mix well pork loin, 3 tablespoons brown sugar, and Cajun seasoning. Toss well to coat. Marinate in the ref for 3 hours.

2 In a medium bowl mix well, brown sugar and vinegar for basting.

3 Thread pork pieces in skewers. Baste with sauce and place on skewer rack in air fryer.

4   Air Frying. For 12 minutes, cook on 360°F.

Halfway through Cooking Time, turnover

skewers and baste with sauce. If needed, cook

in batches.

5   Serve and enjoy.

Nutrition:

Calories: 428;

Fat: 16.7g;

Protein:39g;

Sugar:2g

Pork Loin with Potatoes

Preparation Time: 10 minutes

Cooking Time: 25 minutes

Servings: 2

Ingredients:

- pounds pork loin
- large red potatoes, chopped
- ½ teaspoon garlic powder
- ½ teaspoon red pepper flakes, crushed
- Salt and black pepper, to taste

Directions:

1 In a large bowl, put all of the ingredients together except glaze and toss to coat well. Preheat the Air fryer to 325 degrees F. Place the loin in the air fryer basket.
2 Arrange the potatoes around pork loin.
3 Cook for about 25 minutes.

Nutrition:

Calories:260

Fat: 8g

Carbs: 27g

Protein: 21g

Roasted Char Siew (Pork Butt)

Preparation Time: 10 minutes

Cooking Time: 25 minutes

Servings: 4

Ingredients:

- 1 strip of pork shoulder butt with a good amount of fat marbling
- Marinade:
- 1 tsp. sesame oil
- tbsp. raw honey
- 1 tsp. light soy sauce
- 1 tbsp. rose wine

Directions:

1   Mix all of the marinade ingredients together and put it to a Ziploc bag. Place pork in bag, making sure all sections of pork strip are engulfed in the marinade. Chill 3-24 hours.

2   Take out the strip 30 minutes before planning to cook and preheat your air fryer to 350 degrees.

3   Place foil on small pan and brush with olive oil. Place marinated pork strip onto prepared pan.

4   Set temperature to 350°F, and set time to 20
    minutes. Roast 20 minutes.

5   Glaze with marinade every 5-10 minutes.

6   Remove strip and leave to cool a few minutes
    before slicing.

Nutrition:

Calories: 289;

Fat: 13g;

Protein:33g;

Sugar:1g

Asian Pork Chops

Preparation Time: 2 hours and 10 minutes

Cooking Time: 15 minutes

Servings: 2

Ingredients:

- 1/2 cup hoisin sauce
- tablespoons cider vinegar
- 1 tablespoon Asian sweet chili sauce
- (1/2-inch-thick) boneless pork chops
- salt and pepper

Directions:

1. Stir together hoisin, chili sauce, and vinegar in a large mixing bowl. Separate a quarter cup of this mixture, then add pork chops to the bowl and let it sit in the fridge for 2 hours. Take out the pork chops and place them on a plate. Sprinkle each side of the pork chop evenly with salt and pepper.

2. Cook at 360 degrees for 14 minutes, flipping half way through. Brush with reserved marinade and serve.

Nutrition:

Calories: 338;

Fat: 21g;

Protein:19g;

Fiber:1g

Marinated Pork Chops

Preparation Time: 10 minutes

Cooking Time: 30 minutes

Serve: 2

Ingredients:

- pork chops, boneless
- 1 tsp garlic powder
- ½ cup flour
- 1 cup buttermilk
- Salt and pepper

Directions:

1   Add pork chops and buttermilk in a zip-lock bag. Seal the bag and set aside in the refrigerator overnight.

2   In another zip-lock bag add flour, garlic powder, pepper, and salt.

3   Remove marinated pork chops from buttermilk and add in flour mixture and shake until well coated.

4   Preheat the instant vortex air fryer oven to 380 F.

5   Spray air fryer tray with cooking spray.

6 Arrange pork chops on a tray and air fryer for 28-30 minutes. Turn pork chops after 18 minutes.

7 Serve and enjoy.

Nutrition:

Calories 424

Fat 21.3 g

Carbs 30.8 g

Protein 25.5 g

Steak with Cheese Butter

Preparation Time: 10 minutes

Cooking Time: 8-10 minutes

Servings: 2

Ingredients:

- rib-eye steaks
- tsp garlic powder
- 1/2 tbsp blue cheese butter
- 1 tsp pepper
- tsp kosher salt

Directions:

1 Preheat the air fryer to 400 F.

2 Mix together garlic powder, pepper, and salt and rub over the steaks.

3 Spray air fryer basket with cooking spray.

4 Put the steak in the air fryer basket and cook for 4-5 minutes on each side.

5 Top with blue butter cheese.

6 Serve and enjoy.

Nutrition:

Calories 830

Fat 60 g

Carbohydrates 3 g

Sugar 0 g

Protein 70g

Cholesterol 123 mg

Mussels Bowls

Preparation Time: 5 minutes

Cooking Time: 15 minutes

Servings: 2

Ingredients:

- pounds mussels, scrubbed
- ounces black beer
- 1 yellow onion, chopped
- ounces spicy sausage, chopped
- 1 tablespoon paprika

Directions:

1   Combine all the ingredients in a pan that fits your air fryer.

2   Put the pan in the air fryer and cook at 400 degrees F for 12 minutes.

3   Divide the mussels into bowls, serve, and enjoy!

Nutrition:

Calories 201,

Fat 6,

Fiber 7,

Carbs 17,

Protein 7

Chicken and Peppercorns Mix

Preparation Time: 5 minutes

Cooking Time: 20 minutes

Servings: 2

Ingredients:

- chicken thighs, boneless
- Salt and black pepper to taste
- ½ cup balsamic vinegar
- garlic cloves, minced
- ½ cup soy sauce

Directions:

1. In a container that fits your air fryer, mix the chicken with all the other ingredients and toss.
2. Put the pan in the fryer and cook at 380 degrees F for 20 minutes.
3. Divide everything between plates and serve.

Nutrition:

Calories 261,

Fat 7,

Fiber 5,

Carbs 15,

Protein 16

Salmon Patties

Preparation Time: 10 minutes

Cooking Time: 7 minutes

Servings: 2

Ingredients:

- oz salmon fillet, minced
- 1 lemon, sliced
- 1/2 tsp garlic powder
- 1 egg, lightly beaten
- 1/8 tsp salt

Directions:

1   Add all ingredients except lemon slices into the bowl and mix until well combined.
2   Spray air fryer basket with cooking spray.
3   Place lemon slice into the air fryer basket.
4   Make the equal shape of patties from salmon mixture and place on top of lemon slices into the air fryer basket.
5   Cook at 390 F for 7 minutes.
6   Serve and enjoy.

Nutrition:

Calories 184

Fat 9.2 g

Carbohydrates 1 g

Sugar 0.4 g

Protein 24.9 g

Cholesterol 132 mg

Shrimp with Veggie

Preparation Time: 10 minutes

Cooking Time: 20 minutes

Servings: 2

Ingredients:

- 50 small shrimp
- 1 tbsp Cajun seasoning
- 1 bag of frozen mix vegetables
- 1 tbsp olive oil

Directions:

1. Line air fryer basket with aluminum foil.
2. In a large bowl, set all of the ingredients and toss well.
3. Transfer shrimp and vegetable mixture into the air fryer basket and cook at 350 F for 10 minutes.
4. Toss well and cook for 10 minutes more.
5. Serve and enjoy.

Nutrition:

Calories 101

Fat 4 g

Carbohydrates 14 g

Sugar 1 g

Protein 2 g

Cholesterol 3 mg

Chili Garlic Chicken Wings

Preparation Time: 10 minutes

Cooking Time: 35 minutes

Servings: 2

Ingredients:

- lbs. chicken wings
- tsp seasoned salt
- 1/2 cup coconut flour
- 1/4 tsp garlic powder
- 1/4 tsp chili powder

Directions:

1 Preheat the air fryer to 370 F.

2 In a bowl, put all of the ingredients but the chicken wings and mix well.

3 Add chicken wings into the bowl coat well.

4 Spray air fryer basket with cooking spray.

5 Add the chicken wings by batches into the air fryer basket.

6 Cook for 35-40 minutes. Shake halfway through.

7 Serve and enjoy.

Nutrition:

Calories 440

Fat 17.1 g

Carbohydrates 1 g

Sugar 0.2 g

Protein 65 g

Funky-Garlic and Turkey Breasts

Preparation Time: 10 minutes

Cooking Time: 25 minutes

Servings: 2

Ingredients:

- ½ teaspoon garlic powder
- tablespoons butter
- ¼ teaspoon dried oregano
- 1-pound turkey breasts, boneless
- 1 teaspoon pepper and salt

Directions:

1   Season turkey on both sides generously with garlic, dried oregano, salt and pepper

2   Set your air fryer to sauté mode and add butter, let the butter melt

3   Add turkey breasts and sauté for 2 minutes on each side

4   Lock the lid and select the "Bake/Roast" setting, bake for 15 minutes at 355 degrees F

5   Serve and enjoy

Nutrition:

Calories 223,

Fat 13g,

Carbohydrates 5g,

Protein 19g

Chili Chicken Wings

Preparation Time: 10 minutes

Cooking Time: 35 minutes

Servings: 2

Ingredients:

- ½ cup hot sauce
- ½ cup water
- tbsp butter
- 32 ounces frozen chicken wings
- ½ tsp paprika

Directions:

1   Add all the ingredients into the cook and crisp basket and place the basket inside the air fryer

2   Place the pressure cooker lid on top of the pot and close the pressure valve to the seal position. Set the pressure cooker function to high heat and set the timer for 5 minutes

3   The moment once cooking is done, release the pressure quickly by carefully opening the steamer valve

Serve hot

Nutrition:

Calories 311,

Fat 23g,

Carbohydrates 0g,

Protein 24g

Lemon Drumsticks

Preparation Time: 10 minutes

Cooking Time: 28 minutes

Servings: 2

Ingredients:

- ½ cup hot sauce
- tbsp butter
- ½ cup water
- 1/3 cup lemon juice
- 1-pound drumstick

Directions:

1   Add all the ingredients into the cook and crisp basket and place the basket inside the air fryer

2   Place the pressure cooker lid on top of the pot and close the pressure valve to the seal position. Set the pressure cooker function to high heat and set the timer for 5 minutes

3   Immediately after the cooking is done, release the pressure quickly by carefully opening the steamer valve.

Serve hot

Nutrition:

Calories 414,

Fat 26g,

Carbohydrates 3g,

Protein 42g.

Salsa Verde Chicken

Preparation Time: 5 minutes

Cooking Time: 25 minutes

Servings: 2

Ingredients:

- ounces Salsa Verde
- 1 tablespoon paprika
- 1-pound boneless chicken breasts
- 1 teaspoon ground coriander
- 1 teaspoon cilantro

Directions:

1 Rub the boneless chicken breasts with the paprika, ground black pepper, and cilantro. Set the pressure cooker to "Pressure" mode.

2 Place the boneless chicken into the pressure cooker. Sprinkle the meat with the salsa Verde and stir well.

3 Close the pressure cooker lid and cook for 30 minutes.

4 When the Cooking Time ends, release the pressure and transfer the chicken to the mixing bowl. Shred the chicken well. Serve it.

Nutrition:

Calories: 160

Fat: 4g

Carbs: 5g

Protein: 26g

Madeira Beef

Preparation Time: 5 minutes

Cooking Time: 25 minutes

Servings: 6

Ingredients:

- 1 cup Madeira
- 1 and ½ pounds beef meat, cubed
- Salt and black pepper to the taste
- 1 yellow onion, thinly sliced
- 1 chili pepper, sliced

Directions:

1 Put the reversible rack in the Air fryer, add the baking pan inside and mix all the ingredients in it.
2 Cook on Baking mode at 380 degrees F for 25 minutes, divide the mix into bowls and serve.

Nutrition:

Calories 295,

Fat 16,

Fiber 9,

Carbs 20,

Protein 15.

Creamy Pork and Zucchinis

Preparation Time: 5 minutes

Cooking Time: 25 minutes

Servings: 4

Ingredients:

- 1 and ½ pounds pork stew meat, cubed
- 1 cup tomato sauce
- 1 tablespoon olive oil
- zucchinis, sliced
- Salt and black pepper to the taste

Directions:

1 Put the reversible rack in the Air fryer, add the baking pan inside and mix all the ingredients in it.
2 Cook on Baking mode at 380 degrees F, divide the mix into bowls and serve.

Nutrition:

Calories 284,

Fat 12,

Fiber 9,

Carbs 17,

Protein 12.

Air-fryer Tofu Satay

Preparation Time: 30 minutes

Cooking Time: 25 minutes

Servings: 2

Ingredients:

- 1 block tofu, extra firm
- tbsp. soy sauce
- tsp ginger garlic paste
- 1 tsp sriracha sauce
- 1 tbsp. maple syrup + lime juice

Directions:

1. Mix the maple syrup with lime juice, ginger garlic paste, sriracha, and soy sauce in a food processor or blender. Blend it until smooth.
2. Cut the tofu into strips. Add the puree over the strips and let it marinate for 15 to 30 minutes.
3. Soak 6 bamboo skewers in water while the tofu marinates.
4. With a wire cutter, cut each skewer into two, as a full skewer will not fit inside the air-fryer.
5. Skewer one strip of tofu to each bamboo stick. Peirce it through the uncut side of the skewer.
6. Place the skewers in the air-fryer. Set the temperature to 370 F and let it cook for 15 minutes. You do not have to toss the contents.
7. Serve with peanut butter sauce.

Nutrition:

Calories: 236

Fat: 11g

Carbs: 17g

Protein: 17g

Sticky-Sweet BBQ Tofu

Preparation Time: 10 minutes

Cooking Time: 50 minutes

Servings: 2

Ingredients:

- 1 ½ cups BBQ sauce
- 1 block tofu, extra firm
- Oil for greasing

Directions:

1   Fix the temperature to 400°F and preheat the air-fryer.

2   Press down the tofu and slice it into 1" cubes.

3   Place them on a greased baking sheet.

4   Apply a coat of BBQ sauce and let it cook in the air-fryer for 20 minutes. Keep it aside.

5   Add ½ cup of BBQ sauce into a glass saucepan. The sauce should evenly spread in the pan. Place the cooked tofu cubes on top and add another layer of the sauce on it.

6   Transfer them to the air-fryer again and let it cook for 30 minutes.

7   Enjoy!

Nutrition:

Calories: 173

Fat: 10g

Carbs 9g

Protein: 16g

Veggie Bowl

Preparation Time: 10 minutes

Cooking Time: 30 minutes

Servings: 2

Ingredients:

- cups Brussel sprouts
- cups sweet potato
- tsp garlic powder
- tbsp. soy sauce, low sodium
- Cooking spray

Directions:

1 Place the sweet potatoes in the air-fryer. Add a light layer of oil for tossing.

2 Top it with 1 tsp of garlic powder and toss.

3 Set the temperature to 400 F and cook for 15 minutes. Toss after 5 minutes.

4 Transfer the Brussels sprouts to the cooking basket and spray a layer of oil and the remaining garlic powder. Toss them well and cook at 400 F for 5 minutes.

5 Drizzle some soy sauce and shake to coat the vegetables evenly.

6   Set to the same temperature and cook for 5 minutes. Check it when it hits 2 minutes and toss the contents.

7   Cooking Time will depend on the vegetable. Once the vegetables are done, they will be soft and brown.

Nutrition:

Calories: 261

Fat: 8g

Carbs: 28g

Protein: 14g

Air fried Fish skin

Preparation Time: 10 minutes

Cooking Time: 15 minutes

Servings: 2

Ingredients:

- ½ pound salmon skin
- tbsp. heart-healthy oil
- Salt and pepper, as needed

Directions:

1   Fix the temperature to 400° F and preheat the air-fryer for 5 minutes.

2   Make sure the salmon skin is patted dry.

3   In a bowl, add all components and combine
    well.

4   Transfer the ingredients to the air-fryer basket
    and close it

5   Allow it to cook for 10 minutes at a temperature
    of 400 F.

6   Shake the items halfway through the Cooking
    Time, to make sure that the skin is cooked
    evenly.

Nutrition:

Calories:150

Fat:13

Carbs:3

Protein: 9

Baked Thai fish

Preparation Time: 10 minutes

Cooking Time: 25 minutes

Servings: 2

Ingredients:

- 1 pound cod fillet
- 1 tbsp. lime juice
- ¼ cup of coconut milk
- Salt and pepper, as needed

Directions:

1 Cut the cod fillet into small pieces.

2 Fix the temperature to 325°F and preheat the fryer for 5 minutes.

3 Add all the ingredients to a baking dish and transfer it to an air-fryer.

4 Let it cook for 20 minutes at a temperature of 325 F.

5 Enjoy!

Nutrition:

Calories: 333

Fat: 5g

Carbs: 56g

Protein: 18g

Oven Braised Corned Beef

Preparation Time: 10 minutes

Cooking Time: 55 minutes

Servings: 2

Ingredients:

- 1 medium onion, chopped
- cups of water
- tbsp. Dijon mustard
- pounds corned beef brisket

Directions:

1. Fix the temperature to 400° F and preheat the air-fryer for 5 minutes.

2. Slice the brisket to chunks

3. Add all the ingredients to a baking tray that fits inside the air-fryer.

4. Let it cook for 50 minutes at a temperature of 400 F.

5. Enjoy!

6. Nutrition:

Calories: 320

Fat: 22g

Carbs: 10g

Protein: 21g

Crispy Keto Pork Bites

Preparation Time: 5 minutes

Cooking Time: 25 minutes

Servings: 2

Ingredients:

- 1 medium onion
- ½ pound pork belly
- tbsp. coconut cream
- 1 tbsp. butter
- Salt & pepper, to taste

Directions:

1 Slice the pork belly into even and thin strips

2 The onion has to be diced.

3 Transfer all the ingredients into a mixing bowl and allow it to marinate in the fridge for the next two hours.

4 Fix the temperature to 350 F and preheat the air-fryer for 5 minutes.

5 Keep the pork strips inside the air-fryer and let it cook for 25 minutes at a temperature of 350 F.

6 Enjoy!

Nutrition:

Calories: 448

Fat:42g

Carbs: 2g

Protein: 20g

Soy and Garlic Mushrooms

Preparation Time: 2 hours and 5 minutes

Cooking Time: 25 minutes

Servings: 2

Ingredients:

- pounds mushrooms
- garlic cloves
- ¼ cup coconut amino
- tbsp. olive oil

Directions:

1. Transfer all the ingredients to a dish and combine until well incorporated.
2. Let it marinate for 2 hours in a fridge
3. Fix the temperature to 350 F and preheat for 5 minutes.
4. Transfer the mushrooms to a heatproof dish that can fit in an air-fryer
5. Let it cook for 20 minutes at a temperature of 350 F.
6. Enjoy!

Nutrition:

Calories: 216

Fat:16g

Carbs: 13g

Protein:11g

Crack Chicken

Preparation Time: 5 minutes

Cooking Time: 30 minutes

Servings: 2

Ingredients:

- 1 block cream cheese
- chicken breasts
- slices of bacon
- ¼ cup olive oil
- Salt and pepper

Direction:

1   Fix the temperature to 350 °F and let the air-fryer preheat for 5 minutes

2   In a baking dish that can fit the air-fryer, place the chicken.

3   Apply the cream cheese and olive oil on it. Fry the bacon and crumble it on top of the chicken.

4   Season as needed.

5   Transfer the dish into the air-fryer and cook it for 25 minutes at a temperature of 350 F.

6   Enjoy!

Nutrition:

Calories: 250

Carbs: 14 g

Fat: 19 g

Protein: 22 g

Bullet-proof Beef Roast

Preparation Time: 2 hours

Cooking Time: 2 hours and 5 minutes

Servings: 2

Ingredients:

1. 1 cup of organic beef

2. tbsp. olive oil

3. pounds beef round roast

4. Salt and pepper, to taste

Directions:

- Place all of the ingredients in a resealable bag and let it marinate in the fridge for about two hours.

- Fix the temperature to 400° F and preheat the air-fryer for 5 minutes.

- Place the ingredients in the Ziploc bag in a baking tray that will fit the air-fryer.

- Let it cook for 2 hours at a temperature of 400 F.

- Serve while it is warm.

Nutrition:

Calories: 280

Carbs: 13 g

Fat: 15 g

Protein: 26 g

Air Fried Catfish

Preparation Time: 5 minutes

Cooking Time: 20 minutes

Servings: 2

Ingredients:

- 1 whole egg
- catfish fillets
- ¼ cup almond flour
- Salt and Pepper, to taste
- tbsp. olive oil

Directions:

1 Fix the temperature to 350 F and preheat the air-fryer for 5 minutes.
2 Sprinkle some salt and pepper on the catfish fillet.
3 Beat the eggs, soak the catfish in it and dip it in almond flour.
4 Remove any excess and apply a coat of olive oil on its surface.
5 Transfer the fish to the air-fryer and let it cook for 15 minutes at a temperature of 350 F.
6 Enjoy!

Nutrition:

Calories: 210

Carbs: 9 g

Fat: 11 g

Protein: 17 g

Lemon Fish Fillet

Preparation Time: 5 minutes

Cooking Time: 20 minutes

Servings: 2

Ingredients:

- salmon fish fillets
- ½ cup almond flour
- 1 lemon
- tbsp. vegetable oil
- 1 whole egg

Directions:

1 Fix the temperature to 400° F and preheat the air-fryer for 5 minutes.

2 Season the fish with lemon, salt, pepper and vegetable oil.

3 Beat the egg and soak the fillet in it. Cover the fillet with almond flour.

4 Transfer the fish into the cooking basket and let it cook for 15 minutes at a temperature of 400 F.

5 Enjoy!

Nutrition:

Calories: 230

Carbs: 10 g

Fat: 12 g

Protein: 20 g

Coconut shrimp

Preparation Time: 10 minutes

Cooking Time: 10 minutes

Servings: 2

Ingredients:

- 1 cup coconut, unsweetened and dried
- large shrimps
- 1 cup white flour
- 1 cup egg white
- 1 cup panko breadcrumbs

Directions:

1 Keep the shrimp on some paper towels.

2 Combine the breadcrumbs and coconut in a pan and keep it aside.

3 In another pan, mix the cornstarch and the flour and keep it aside.

4 Keep the egg whites in a bowl

5 Put the shrimp, one at a time, first in the flour mixture. Then dip it in the egg whites and finally into the breadcrumbs mixture.

6 Transfer all the shrimp into the air-fryer basket.

7 Adjust the temperature to 400 F and time to 10 minutes.

8 Halfway through the Cooking Time, you can turn over the shrimp if needed.

9 Enjoy!

Nutrition:

Calories: 220

Carbs: 11 g

Fat: 10 g

Protein: 16 g

Buffalo wings

Preparation Time: 5 minutes

Cooking Time: 30 minutes

Servings: 2

Ingredients:

- tbsp. hot sauce
- lb. chicken wings
- tbsp. melted butter
- Salt and pepper, to taste

Directions:

- Cut off the ends of the chicken wings

- Mix the hot sauce and melted butter.
- Let the chicken marinate in the hot sauce overnight or for several hours in the fridge.
- Set the temperature to 390 F and preheat the air-fryer
- Transfer the wings into the cooking basket and let it cook for 14 minutes.
- Make the extra sauce with 3 tbsp. of melted butter and ¼ cup of hot sauce.
- Take a plastic bag or a bowl and add the chicken wings to it. Add some extra sauce if necessary.
- Serve with blue cheese dip or ranch.

Nutrition:

Calories: 190

Carbs: 9 g

Fat: 9 g

Protein: 15 g

Rib Eye Steak

Preparation Time: 5 minutes

Cooking Time: 25 minutes

Servings: 2

Ingredients:

1   1 tbsp. olive oil

2   pounds rib eye steak

3   1 tbsp. steak rub

Directions:

- Adjust the Cooking Time of the air-fryer to 4 minutes and then set the temperature to 400 F to preheat.
- Rub both sides of the steak with the rub and olive oil.
- Transfer the steak into the air fry basket.
- Set the Cooking Time to 14 minutes and temperature to 400 F.
- Once 7 minutes is done, turn the steak to its other side.
- When the cooking is done, remove the steak from the fryer and let it cool down for 10 minutes before serving.

Nutrition:

Calories: 310

Carbs: 16 g

Fat: 19 g

Protein: 34 g

Delicious Hot Steaks

Preparation Time: 5 minutes

Cooking Time: 10 minutes

Servings: 2

Ingredients:

1   steaks, 1-inch thick

2   ½ tsp black pepper

3   1 tbsp olive oil

4   ½ tsp ground paprika

5   Salt and black pepper to taste

Directions

- Warm up the air fryer to 390° F. Mix olive oil, black pepper, paprika, salt and pepper and rub onto steaks. Spread evenly. Put the steaks in the fryer, and cook for 6 minutes, turning them halfway through.

Nutrition:

Calories: 300

Carbs: 15 g

Fat: 19 g

Protein: 32 g

Creamy Beef Liver Cakes

Preparation Time: 5 minutes

Cooking Time: 20 minutes

Servings: 2

Ingredients:

1   1 lb beef liver, sliced

2   large eggs

3   1 tbsp butter

4   ½ tbsp black truffle oil

5   1 tbsp cream

6   Salt and black pepper

Directions

- Preheat the Air Fryer to 320 F. Cut the liver into thin slices and refrigerate for 10 minutes. Separate the whites from the yolks and put each yolk in a cup. In another bowl, add the cream, truffle oil, salt and pepper and mix with a fork. Arrange half of the mixture in a small ramekin.

- Pour the white of the egg and divide it equally between ramekins. Top with the egg yolks. Surround each yolk with a liver. Cook for 15 minutes and serve cool.

Nutrition:

Calories: 215

Carbs: 11 g

Fat: 10 g

Protein: 20 g

Pork Chops in Cream

Preparation Time: 5 minutes

Cooking Time: 20 minutes

Servings: 4

Ingredients:

- pork chops, center-cut
- tbsp flour
- tbsp sour cream
- Salt and black pepper

- ½ cup breadcrumbs

Directions

1 Coat the chops with flour. Drizzle the cream over and rub gently to coat well. Spread the breadcrumbs onto a bowl, and coat each pork chop with crumbs. Spray the chops with oil and arrange them in the basket of your Air Fryer. Cook for 14 minutes at 380 F, turning once halfway through. Serve with salad, slaw or potatoes.

Nutrition:

Calories: 250

Carbs: 13 g

Fat: 13 g

Protein: 24 g

Five Spice Pork Belly

Preparation Time: 10 minutes

Cooking Time: 3 hours

Servings: 2

Ingredients:

- 1 ½ lb pork belly, blanched
- 1 tsp five spice seasoning
- ½ tsp white pepper
- ¾ tsp garlic powder
- 1 tsp salt

Directions

1   After blanching the pork belly leave it at room temperature for 2 hours to air dry. Pat with paper towels if there is excess water. Preheat the air fryer to 330 F. Take a skewer and pierce the skin as many times as you can, so you can ensure crispiness. Combine the seasonings in a small bowl, and rub it onto the pork.

2   Place the pork into the air fryer and cook for 30 minutes. Heat up to 350 F and cook for 30 more minutes. Let cool slightly before serving.

Nutrition:

Calories: 280

Carbs: 14 g

Fat: 17 g

Protein: 29 g

Fast Rib Eye Steak

Preparation Time: 5 minutes

Cooking Time: 10 minutes

Servings: 2

Ingredients:

- pounds rib eye steak
- 1 tbsp olive oil
- Salt and black pepper to taste

Directions

1   Preheat your fryer to 350 F. Rub both sides of the steak with oil; season with salt and pepper. Place the steak in your Air Fryer's cooking basket and cook for 8 minutes. Serve and enjoy!

Nutrition:

Calories: 300

Carbs: 15 g

Fat: 19 g

Protein: 32 g

Pork Tenderloins with Apple

Preparation Time: 5 minutes

Cooking Time: 50 minutes

Servings: 4

Ingredients:

- pork tenderloins
- 1 apple, wedged
- 1 cinnamon quill
- 1 tbsp soy sauce
- Salt and black pepper

Directions

1 In a bowl, add pork, apple, cinnamon, soy sauce, salt, and black pepper into; stir to coat well. Let sit at room temperature for 25-35 minutes. Put the pork and apples into the air fryer, and a little bit of marinade. Cook at 380 F for 14 minutes, turning once halfway through. Serve hot!

Nutrition:

Calories: 200

Carbs: 10 g

Fat: 10 g

Protein: 18 g

Awesome Beef Bulgogi with Mushrooms

Preparation Time: 3 hours

Cooking Time: 20 minutes

Servings: 2

Ingredients:

- oz beef
- ½ cup sliced mushrooms
- tbsp bulgogi marinade
- 1 tbsp diced onion

Directions

1   Slice the beef into bite-size pieces and place them in a bowl. Add the bulgogi and mix to coat the beef completely. Cover the bowl and place in the fridge for 3 hours to marinate. Preheat the air fryer to 350 F.

2   Transfer the beef to a baking dish; stir in the mushroom and onion. Cook for 10 minutes, until nice and tender. Serve with some roasted potatoes and a green salad.

Nutrition:

Calories: 220

Carbs: 12 g

Fat: 11 g

Protein: 23 g

Homemade Beef Liver Soufflé

Preparation Time: 15 minutes

Cooking Time: 30 minutes

Servings: 2

Ingredients:

- ½ lb of beef liver
- eggs
- oz buns
- 1 cup warm milk
- Salt and black pepper to taste

Directions

1 Cut the liver in slices and put it in the fridge for 15 minutes. Divide the buns into pieces and soak them in milk for 10 minutes. Put the liver in a blender, and add the yolks, the bread mixture, and the spices. Grind the components and stuff in the ramekins. Line the ramekins in the Air Fryer's basket; cook for 20 minutes at 350 F.

Nutrition:

Calories: 230

Carbs: 15 g

Fat: 11 g

Protein: 26 g

Authentic Wiener Beef Schnitzel

Preparation Time: 5 minutes

Cooking Time: 30 minutes

Servings: 4

Ingredients:

1   beef schnitzel cutlets

2   ½ cup flour

3   eggs, beaten

4   Salt and black pepper

5   1 cup breadcrumbs

Directions

- Coat the beef cutlets in flour and take away any excess. Dip the coated cutlets into the egg mixture. Season it with salt and black pepper. Then dip it into the crumbs and coat well. Drizzle them generously with oil and cook for 10 minutes at 360 F, turning once halfway through.

Nutrition:

Calories: 195

Carbs: 12 g

Fat: 11 g

Protein: 18 g

Herbed Beef Roast

Preparation Time: 5 minutes

Cooking Time: 45 minutes

Servings: 2

Ingredients:

- tsp olive oil
- 1 lb. beef Roast
- ½ tsp dried rosemary
- ½ tsp dried oregano
- Salt and black pepper to taste

Directions

1   Preheat the Air Fryer to 400 F. Drizzle oil over the beef, and sprinkle with salt, pepper, and herbs. Rub onto the meat with hands. Cook for 45 minutes for medium-rare and 50 minutes for well-done.

2   Check halfway through, and flip to ensure they cook evenly. Wrap the beef in foil for 10 minutes after cooking to allow the juices to reabsorb into the meat. Slice the beef and serve with a side of steamed asparagus.

Nutrition:

Calories: 235

Carbs: 12 g

Fat: 13 g

Protein: 28 g

Effortless Beef Schnitzel

Preparation Time: 5 minutes

Cooking Time: 20 minutes

Servings: 2

Ingredients:

- tbsp vegetable oil
- oz breadcrumbs
- 1 whole egg, whisked
- 1 thin beef schnitzel, cut into strips
- 1 whole lemon

Directions

1 Preheat your fryer to 356 F. In a bowl, add breadcrumbs and oil and stir well to get a loose mixture. Dip schnitzel in egg, then dip in breadcrumbs coat well. Place the prepared schnitzel your Air Fryer's cooking basket and cook for 12 minutes. Serve with a drizzle of lemon juice.

Nutrition:

Calories: 205

Carbs: 12 g

Fat: 11 g

Protein: 25 g

Sweet Marinated Pork Chops

Preparation Time: 5 minutes

Cooking Time: 20 minutes

Servings: 3

Ingredients:

- pork chops, ½-inch thick
- Salt and black pepper to taste
- 1 tbsp maple syrup
- 1 ½ tbsp minced garlic
- tbsp mustard

Directions

1 In a bowl, add all ingredients except the pork, and mix well. Add the pork and toss it in the mustard sauce to coat well. Slide-out the fryer basket and place the chops in the basket; cook at 350 F for 6 minutes.

2 Halfway through, flip the pork and cook further for 6 minutes. Once ready, remove them onto a serving platter and serve with a side of steamed asparagus.

Nutrition:

Calories: 260

Carbs: 13 g

Fat: 15 g

Protein: 27 g

Sage Sausages Balls

Preparation Time: 5 minutes

Cooking Time: 20 minutes

Servings: 4

Ingredients:

- ½ oz sausages, sliced
- Salt and black pepper to taste
- 1 cup onion, chopped
- tbsp breadcrumbs
- 1 tsp sage

Directions

1   Heat up your Air Fryer to 340 F. In a bowl, mix onions, sausage meat, sage, salt and pepper. Add breadcrumbs to a plate. Form balls using the mixture and roll them in breadcrumbs. Add onion balls in your Air Fryer's cooking basket and cook for 15 minutes. Serve and enjoy!

Nutrition:

Calories: 185

Carbs: 10 g

Fat: 11 g

Protein: 17 g

Pork Belly with Honey

Preparation Time: 5 minutes

Cooking Time: 30 minutes

Servings: 8

Ingredients:

- pounds pork belly
- ½ tsp pepper
- 1 tbsp olive oil
- 1 tbsp salt
- tbsp honey

Directions

1 Preheat your Air Fryer to 400 F. Season the pork belly with salt and pepper. Grease the basket with oil. Add seasoned meat and cook for 15 minutes. Add honey and cook for 10 minutes more. Serve with green salad.

Nutrition:

Calories: 250

Carbs: 12 g

Fat: 14 g

Protein: 25 g

Cocktail Franks in Blanket

Preparation Time: 5 minutes

Cooking Time: 20 minutes

Servings: 4

Ingredients:

- oz cocktail franks
- oz can crescent rolls

Directions

1   Use a paper towel to pat the cocktail franks to drain completely. Cut the dough in 1 by 1.5-inch rectangles using a knife. Gently roll the franks in the strips, making sure the ends are visible Place in freezer for 5 minutes.

2   Preheat the fryer to 330 F. Take the franks out of the freezer and place them in the air fryer's basket and cook for 6-8 minutes. Increase the temperature to 390 F. cook for another 3 minutes until a fine golden texture appears.

Nutrition:

Calories: 170

Carbs: 10 g

Fat: 10 g

Protein: 16 g

Seasoned Pork Shoulder

Preparation Time: 15 minutes

Cooking Time: 1 hour

Servings: 10

Ingredients:

- pounds skin-on, bone-in pork shoulder
- 2-3 tablespoons adobo seasoning
- Salt, as required

Directions:

1. Arrange the pork shoulder onto a cutting board, skin-side down.
2. Season the inner side of pork shoulder with adobo seasoning and salt.
3. Season the inner side of pork shoulder with salt and adobo seasoning
4. With kitchen twines, tie the pork shoulder into a long round cylinder shape.
5. Season the outer side of pork shoulder with salt.
6. Insert the rotisserie rod through the pork shoulder.

7   Insert the rotisserie forks, one on each side of the rod to secure the pork shoulder.

8   Arrange the drip pan in the bottom of Instant Omni Plus Toaster Oven.

9   Now, slide the rod's left side into the groove along the metal bar so it doesn't move.

10 Then, close the door and touch "Rotate".

11 Select "Roast" and then adjust the temperature to 350 degrees F.

12 Set the timer for 60 minutes and press the "Start".

13 When Cooking Time is complete, press the red lever to release the rod.

14 Remove the pork from toaster oven and place onto a platter for about 10 minutes before slicing.

15 With a knife, slice the pork shoulder into desired sized slices and serve.

Nutrition:

Calories 397

Total Fat 29.1 g

Saturated Fat 10.7 g

Cholesterol 122 mg

Sodium 176 mg

Total Carbs 0 g

Fiber 0 g

Sugar 0 g

Protein 31.7 g

30-Day Meal Plan

Day	Breakfast	Lunch/dinner	Dessert
1	Shrimp Skillet	Spinach Rolls	Matcha Crepe Cake
2	Coconut Yogurt with Chia Seeds	Goat Cheese Fold-Overs	Pumpkin Spices Mini Pies
3	Chia Pudding	Crepe Pie	Nut Bars
4	Egg Fat Bombs	Coconut Soup	Pound Cake
5	Morning "Grits"	Fish Tacos	Tortilla Chips with Cinnamon Recipe
6	Scotch Eggs	Cobb Salad	Granola Yogurt with Berries
7	Bacon Sandwich	Cheese Soup	Berry Sorbet

8	Noatmeal	Tuna Tartare	Coconut Berry Smoothie
9	Breakfast Bake with Meat	Clam Chowder	Coconut Milk Banana Smoothie
10	Breakfast Bagel	Asian Beef Salad	Mango Pineapple Smoothie
11	Egg and Vegetable Hash	Keto Carbonara	Raspberry Green Smoothie
12	Cowboy Skillet	Cauliflower Soup with Seeds	Loaded Berries Smoothie
13	Feta Quiche	Prosciutto-Wrapped Asparagus	Papaya Banana and Kale Smoothie
14	Bacon Pancakes	Stuffed Bell Peppers	Green Orange Smoothie

15	Waffles	Stuffed Eggplants with Goat Cheese	Double Berries Smoothie
16	Chocolate Shake	Korma Curry	Energizing Protein Bars
17	Eggs in Portobello Mushroom Hats	Zucchini Bars	Sweet and Nutty Brownies
18	Matcha Fat Bombs	Mushroom Soup	Keto Macho Nachos
19	Keto Smoothie Bowl	Stuffed Portobello Mushrooms	Peanut Butter Choco Banana Gelato with Mint
20	Salmon Omelet	Lettuce Salad	Cinnamon Peaches and Yogurt
21	Hash Brown	Onion Soup	Pear Mint Honey Popsicles

22	Black's Bangin' Casserole	Asparagus Salad	Orange and Peaches Smoothie
23	Bacon Cups	Cauliflower Tabbouleh	Coconut Spiced Apple Smoothie
24	Spinach Eggs and Cheese	Beef Salpicao	Sweet and Nutty Smoothie
25	Taco Wraps	Stuffed Artichoke	Ginger Berry Smoothie
26	Coffee Donuts	Spinach Rolls	Vegetarian Friendly Smoothie
27	Egg Baked Omelet	Goat Cheese Fold-Overs	ChocNut Smoothie
28	Ranch Risotto	Crepe Pie	Coco Strawberry Smoothie
29	Scotch Eggs	Coconut Soup	Egg Spinach Berries Smoothie

30	Fried Eggs	Fish Tacos	Creamy Dessert Smoothie

Conclusion

Thanks for making it to the end of this book. An air fryer is a relatively new addition to the kitchen, and it's easy to see why people are getting excited about using it. With an air fryer, you can make crispy fries, chicken wings, chicken breasts and steaks in minutes. There are many delicious foods that you can prepare without adding oil or grease to your meal. Again make sure to read the instructions on your air fryer and follow the rules for proper usage and maintenance. Once your air fryer is in good working condition, you can really get creative and start experimenting your way to healthy food that tastes great.

That's it! Thank you!

CPSIA information can be obtained
at www.ICGtesting.com
Printed in the USA
BVHW061809230321
603273BV00004B/327